BEAT THE BOSS

A Roleplaying Game for Organizing on the Job
and in the Community

D0036815

BEAT THE BOSS

A Roleplaying Game for Organizing on the Job
and in the Community

Doug Geisler

Practical Fox LLC

Beat the Boss
First Edition

Practical Fox, Portland Oregon
© Doug Geisler
All rights reserved.
First edition published 2019.
Cover image by Sherman, Nathan, Artist.
Work With Care. , 1936. [Pennsylvania: Federal Art Project] Photograph. https://www.loc.gov/item/98517388/.
Cover design by Carly Cohen
Illustrations by Xavier Lopez Gama
Editing and production by Practical Fox
Paperback ISBN: 978-1-7320603-0-2
eBook ISBN: 978-1-7320306-1-9
Library of Congress Control Number: 2018966239

CONTENTS

CHAPTER 1

Let Me Introduce Myself on This Cut

I started playing roleplaying games in middle school. I ran my half-elf ranger all over the home-brew worlds that my friends made up. I learned then that imaginary scenarios carry weight—not equal to lived experience, but experiences all their own. I got a degree in anthropology in college and in doing so read many monographs on different cultures and subcultures. When I got my first jobs in food service, I quickly learned firsthand what my value was as a worker and that each workplace had a culture. When I got the opportunity to organize workers after the Seattle WTO protests in 1999, I found out that the best way that organizers train to go talk to workers was the same tool I'd used since middle school. You have a hard conversation coming up? Roleplay it out so you're prepared.

I wrote this game after having struggled through over fifteen years of union organizing. The trainings I've gone to didn't give an opportunity to the trainees to make all the decisions about a campaign and live with the circumstances. Usually once the campaign training starts, it's on a set of rails that steer organizers toward an eventual outcome. This game gives you the opportunity to test out new tactics and strategies.

Children are being used as political pawns by Republican sociopaths. We've forgotten as Americans how many soldiers are currently in war zones. Capitalists are working tirelessly to undermine the only tool that has proven successful at rebalancing their control of democracy—unions. If we as activists don't try something, anything new, everything we stand for is going to be illegal. Activists need a playground. Welcome to *Beat the Boss*.

This game is for every variety of organizer. It could be used by the Industrial Areas Foundation, the Rural Organizing Project, and every union. It offers practice in game form for oppressed people all over: fast food workers, grocery clerks, bank tellers—anybody. If you've got a job, you are being taken advantage of and need to learn some organizing skills.

This game is also for any roleplayer. In the last few years, it has become clear that we are everywhere. Well-crafted games give a peek into the sociopolitical existence of a wide variety of people. Roleplaying games stretch the empathy muscle in everyone.

Have fun!

I encourage my union organizing colleagues who pull together training materials for organizing in their own locals and industries to use this system to train organizers by adapting current materials.

> *A word on gender and pronouns: I chose not to use "sex" as the descriptor because that is often an inexact term for the panoply of likes and shapes that organizers and workers can express themselves in. As you know better, do better, and all that.*

If you've played a roleplaying game before, jump straight to chapter 2, make a character, and starting smashing capitalism.

If you are new to roleplaying games, keep reading, even if it seems a touch complex. Union organizing seems like complex legal wizardry from outside, but it is amazingly simple for workers with the same employer to come together and demand changes. In both real-life organizing and *Beat the Boss*, as long as you are having fun and telling your own story, you are doing it right. The rules for this game should not get in your way.

If you are a seasoned gamer of games, this game may feel like it's railroading the players. While the overall narrative for workers who are organizing is similar to a linear story, there is a great deal of latitude in the plotline. The interaction between characters and the game system creates great fiction. Play on.

If you've played Powered by the Apocalypse before, the dice rolling mechanic, the players' declaration of actions, the GM's suggestions for the use of moves, and everyone's participation in creating the narrative will feel familiar. Some of the mechanisms are borrowed from other Powered by the Apocalypse games, and some problems in this game needed to be solved by new systems. Look at the Majority, Regard, Marks, and Stages rules for more details.

What Is This?

Beat the Boss is a roleplaying game, a training tool, and the seeds of the revolution. You and your friends or colleagues are going to gather to talk. You're going to tell a story about some workers you meet and how you help them win their very own union or solve their community's problems. You'll make characters that are totally fictional, or the characters could be near replicas of yourselves. These characters will talk through their efforts to educate workers and plan for the campaign to help the workers win. They may closely resemble yourself while you train—in a safe environment—for skills that you can take into the field and use to help workers solve their problems.

The rules will guide and shape the story you tell. There will be dice, and dice are fickle.

The Boss:

You have one. If you're lucky, you've *had* one. A Boss is the person making the most money off of the surplus value that your work produces. Bosses decide how the workplace is run. Is it for the workers' benefit? Or is it run for the Boss's benefit? If you and your friends are running a game that focuses on community organizing, you will be directing all of the organizing toward the Decision Maker. The Decision Maker is responsible for the ills in your community.

The Union Buster:

They're the highly paid lawyer hired by the Boss to keep the employer union-free. It's usually a formerly middling law student who puts their training in creating a sense of doubt among a jury to use by creating a sense of doubt among workers. The Busters are most effective when they resemble the workers they are lying to, so they will likely match the demographics of the workforce.

They will introduce chaos and hardship. Chaos and hardship will introduce innovation and novelty. Innovation will allow for small and large triumphs. You play the game to find out what happens.

There is opposition. Very few workers get it together well enough to build a union that can win material change for themselves and their families. It is rare for workers in America to know what a union really is. In 2017 10.7 percent of workers were in an organized union, per the US Bureau of Labor Statistics. The number of wage and salary workers belonging to unions, at 14.8 million in 2017, edged up by 262,000 from 2016. In 1983, the first year for which comparable union data are available, the union membership rate was 20.1 percent. Media doesn't create the expectation that together people can win. Bosses (in workplace organizing) and Decision Makers (in community issue organizing) certainly don't want people to learn that standing together works. Sometimes organizations get in their own way when people want to change the balance of power between themselves and their employer in their working lives.

Workers spend eight to twelve hours a day doing some activity that they trade for money. People exist in a web of interactions giving care and receiving care, providing and consuming. Most things—food, water, electricity, rent, gasoline, car insurance, clothing, entertainment, health insurance, and hand-tooled leather dice bags—cost so much that whatever people do manage to take home from that work is stretched very thin. This game is about union organizing. Organizing creates a dramatic tension between fear and ego, survival and respect, control and power.

Beat the Boss puts you in the role of the organizer in a struggle for social and economic justice. The bulk of the action takes place in the most normal of places: living rooms

> This rule set is based on Vincent Baker's *Apocalypse World* and really inspired by *Night Witches* by Jason Morningstar. If you've played those two or any of the other Powered by the Apocalypse games, you'll get it quick.

and dining rooms. Organizers talk to workers about hope and the future. If you use this game for training, you'll use your own rap for the conversation and other players will fill in for the workers.

The rules are made to reflect the real hardship of workers coming together. Each Campaign Stage is full of opportunities for workers to turn back from their higher selves and remain in their self-interested silos isolated from the community around them. Organizers are marked by the anger, fear, and frustration that swirls in clouds around workers fighting bosses.

WHAT YOU NEED

Beat the Boss requires at least two players. Five is probably the best number. If the group grows larger than that, you may come across some difficulties, like boredom for the players and mania for the GM.

One player is the game master, or GM. That person should read the GM chapter of the game. If you run *Beat the Boss* over the long haul, it won't be a problem for people to come and go. That is the nature of the work of organizers.

You'll also need comfortable places to sit for a time. This game is potentially episodic and can be played over lunch breaks to keep the team sharp between campaigns, or you can play in two-hour sessions after work. The game or training you and your friends play can run from first contact all the way to ratifying a collective bargaining agreement or celebrating the resolution of a community problem. You can pick out the Campaign Stages that reflect the work that your fellow organizers are doing now in order to puzzle through an encounter with a challenging worker.

You are definitely going to need dice, pencils, and paper. You may also need something to use for tracking the Campaign Pool (coins, poker chips, etc.).

ADULT CONTENT

Organizing occurs with many workers who use adult language. Sometimes organizers hook up. Sometimes organizing is done on the road, where the team stays at a hotel. Stuff happens.

I suggest you incorporate agreements on the boundaries of the game at the outset. If you are playing *Beat the Boss* at work, be aware of the topics that may be, as the saying goes, not suitable for work. Use the "X Card" if appropriate for your table.

The X Card
Because of the improvisational nature of rpgs (role-playing games) and larps (live-action roleplaying), we don't always know what will happen until it happens. It's possible that the game could go in a direction that would make people feel uncomfortable. The X-Card, created by John Stavropoulos, allows anyone (including the GM) to edit out content mid-game and resolve issues as they arise.

—Big Bad Con 2018

THE CONVERSATION

The whole game is just you and your friends talking. But that's roleplaying: asking questions and using the answers to propel the action. The other mechanics are here to create obstacles. No one would be moved by *The Lord of the Rings* if Frodo popped the ring in the mail, dusted off his hands, and went back to doing hobbit things. Challenges and problems are endemic in life and very much evident in organizing. You and your friends will create the scenes, use the questions, and play your way to the answers.

SCENES

For each public action led by workers, there are hours of down time. For each Housevisit that recruits the Primerx to the campaign, there are hours of driving between empty houses. *Beat the Boss* is a game, and it would do pretty bad at its job of entertaining if you and your friends played out the boring shit. You all will hand wave that stuff to get to the action. If the GM asserts that the steps you take as an organizer just work, go with it. Sometimes you invent something too perfect for the story to allow a roll of the dice to foul it up.

Your scenes will be set depending on the Campaign Stage and the questions that you'd like to answer then. It's acceptable for the GM to not be the only one asking questions. Everyone in the game should get a chance at GMing. If you have a question about the way a character is acting or what they are saying, others may be curious too. Ask away.

You could get really deeply engrossed in the little details of organizing. Sometimes success in organizing comes down to the details, but that may not be the goal of your game. There are many ways to get to the goals of a group of workers, and there are many ways to roleplay.

If you haven't played a roleplaying game before, think of your storytelling as if it was a movie scene. Describing camera angles, lighting, set design, and actors cast in different roles can give you a foundation to tell the story you want.

MOVES

The conversation will eventually come to a point when there is an event that has a chance of failing. Then you, the player, will pull a move out of your hat. Look over your playbook and find the move that best fits the scene. You can try to steer the story so that a move is applicable and then let the GM decide if it applies. Do what the move tells you to and let things get interesting (not necessarily fun, but interesting, which is its own kind of fun).

There are several types of moves: Organizing (outward facing work), Campaign (internal facing work), Special, Boss, and Tendency moves. Any player will do two moves per campaign day. These can be in any combination of one Organizing and one Campaign move. Each Tendency has its own moves that make it stand apart. The Tendency moves can replace the Campaign or Organizing moves or be played as needed in the game.

Chapter 3 has all the details on moves any organizer can use.

Rolling Dice

When a move requires that you roll dice, you will roll two six-sided dice [noted as 2d6] and add the results together, along with the +[Stat] noted. If you have any Regard for the subject of the move, you will add +1 or -1 to the roll. Some moves and GM actions call for rolling one six-sided die [1d6] to determine a result.

If your organizer earns "+1 forward," that means she adds one to her next relevant roll. This bonus is used only once, and it may be conditional, situational, or time limited. There is one exception to this rule: the roleplaying bonus elected by the players during a Recruit, Repair a Relationship, or Housevisit move. If the players feel that the performance warrants an additional bonus, it can stack on top of other bonuses.

If your organizer earns a hold, that is a bonus that can be used now or in the future, whenever it makes sense. Holds do not stack, so you can't apply three of them at once.

If the result is a ten or more, your organizer will succeed at the test with no hassles.

If the result is a six or less, the character is not going to succeed. It may really suck for them. The GM will make sure that you, the player, don't like the outcome. You have handed the GM a golden opportunity to complicate your game.

If the result is between seven and nine, you succeed (yay) but at a cost (boo). The most dramatic and narratively exciting results lie here. The GM will offer you some bargain, or you will be able to propose your own result. For most moves, there will be a few options to help you make choices appropriate for the situation.

CHAPTER 2

Creating Your Character

STATS

Skill is a measure of academic training, union training, and assiduous attention to detail. It is most useful for Recruiting a Primerx and Housevisiting any worker. You must put all of the things you've learned in training to use when attempting to overcome the hesitations of the worker.

> **Primerx**
> The A-number-one leader of any group of workers. This worker is the leader of other leaders. They can be male or female, so this book uses the handy gender-neutral "x" ending, as in Latinx. The Primerx carries 1 forward to Repairing Relationships and counts as two leaders for all calculations regarding Support.

Vigor is a measure of stamina, endurance, and toughness. Organizers rely on guts to last through long days of Housevisiting, standing in the parking lot or outside of the worksite flyering, or preparing and leading a group of workers to march on the Boss.

Smarts is a measure of raw talent and sharpness of mind. Smarts come in handy when you chart the workplace to look for the pattern in the assessments or when you imagine the snags and hurdles that may come to pass when planning an action.

Empathy is a measure of an organizer's way with workers and the community. A low Empathy score leaves an organizer cold to others' problems, while an organizer rich in Empathy connects with people easily and deeply. Workers trust an Empathetic organizer easily.

Moxie is the measure of personal courage and determination in the face of social, political, or economic pressure to act otherwise. Organizers call upon Moxie to show no fear when tempting fate. The odds of workers organizing in modern America are stacked against success, and organizers will need plenty of Moxie to move the Boss.

SENIORITY

Even at the start of the game, you can choose a seniority level to reflect your character's years of experience. You can opt to be an organizer-in-training (OIT), organizer, or senior organizer.

- Senior organizers can add a total of +2 to Skill, Vigor, Smarts, Empathy, and Moxie (Eg. +0, +1, -1, +2, +0 or +0, +2, +0, +0, +0). All stats have a hard cap of +3.
- Organizers can add a total of +1 to stats.
- Organizers-in-training (OIT) start with a total of 0 in stats.

TENDENCIES

There are common habits that many organizers fall into. These grow out of past organizer experiences and are often either reinforcements of things that were done to garner a win or scars from things that were done in a campaign that lost. The Tendencies are not wrong or right as applied to organizing workers. Players will choose a Tendency for their organizer. More than one player can opt for the same Tendency, but for creating drama and interest in game play, the Game Master can use a subtle nudge to help the players choose differences among the Tendencies.

Each Tendency has moves that are unique to it and reinforce their strengths and weaknesses. Each organizer will begin play with two moves chosen from their Tendency. Organizers can choose more moves as they gain experience throughout the campaign.

Labor Organizer

When faced with organizing options or threats from the Boss, the labor organizer will act on the instinct to follow the written plan and do the next thing in the "steps to winning a union" diagram—damn the consequences. This tendency believes the system is rigged against workers winning a thing from the coffers of the rich. She knows unions succeeded in the past by doing three things—getting a list, recruiting an organizing committee, and showing no fear—and so will she.

Moves

Ghosts of Campaigns Past

You enjoy a +1 when redoing any task or move that failed in a previous Organizing Stage.

Union Thug

The inner fire of the labor movement burns within you. You can call upon this vigor to pull off a move that you aren't built for. Choose a single Campaign or Organizing move. Replace the rolled stat with +[Vigor] when you trigger it. You can choose this multiple times, but it must be applied to a different move each time.

Use Existing Law to Make the Boss Bend

Almost all Bosses break the law: wage and hour laws, labor laws, health and safety rules, consumer regulations, or something else, depending on the industry. If the workers present proof or the Boss uses a move that opens him up to legal action, roll +[Smarts]. On a 10 or higher, force the Boss to spend 20 Public Capital by calling the correct enforcement agency to make a visit to the shop. On a 7–9, the Boss must spend 10 Cash defending themselves and choose two:

- You file incomplete paperwork.
- The worker misrepresented the relevant facts.
- The punishment is not meaningful.
- Take a Harm for your effort.

On a 6 or less, your effort is wasted, and you will be asked to answer for it by the Organizing Director.

Hearings Master

During the course of many campaigns, Union Busters will divert much of the building energy of the workers into legal avenues. A hearing by the National Labor Relations Board (NLRB) can be resolved quickly, or appeals can drag out after the election takes place. Roll +[Skill] when the campaign is brought to a labor relations board hearing. On a 10 or higher, the issues raised by the Boss are resolved without complication. On a 7–9, the hearing happens in a timely fashion and choose one:

- Some workers are determined to be out of the unit. Which organizing committee member (OC) do you lose?
- Some workers are determined to be added to the unit. Lose 10% of your support.
- The vote can move forward, but issues will arise during negotiations. What are they?

On a 6 or less, your hearing will delay the vote, giving the Boss 1d6 extra shifts prior to the vote day to spend Cash to erode your support.

Know the Plan, Live the Plan

Your campaign plan is well thought out, and you exude confidence in your visits with workers. To recruit a worker, you don't need to finish a Housevisit if you instead take a Mark or 1 Harm, your choice.

Choose a move from any other Tendency

Look and Background

Choose **one** from each category.

Gender & Sexuality (choose as you feel appropriate): CIS, L, G, B, T, Q, I, ?, ___, ___, ___, ___

Preferred Pronoun:

Clothes: Business casual, Union T-shirt and Slacks, Cushioned, Dependable, American-made, _____

Body: Big-boned, Heavy, Wiry, Sinewy, Petite, Lush, _____

Eyes: Kind, Bleary, Hard, Round, Protruding, ____

Who you relate to outside of the union: Married Partner, Ex-coworker, Friend at Another Union, _____

Vehicle: Shiny, Sedan, Road-dusted, _____

COMMUNITY ORGANIZER

This organizer builds power by bringing people together—lots of people. A community organizer's tendency is to go big with their outreach. It is great for movement building. At this time, the labor movement desperately needs a movement of supporters walking with them, but the community organizer sometimes tries to broaden their audience beyond the workers at the workplace that is organizing.

Moves
People's Hero
Name the politico that has taken a personal interest in your career. The personality may

represent a city, county, state, or federal position. The organizer gets to determine the rank and name of the politico. In order to bring the politico into play in the game, roll +[Moxie]. On a 10 or higher, the politico comes in as planned. On a 7–9, the GM gets to present a bargain for the politico's participation in the campaign. On a 6 or less, the politico has a scheduling conflict and is unavailable.

Everyone's Friend

When faced with your failure during a debrief or performance evaluation, also add +[Empathy] to rolls shit talking you or when the organizing director evaluates your performance.

Shared Concerns

You know how to connect with people's issues and cares. You seamlessly relate to them. Choose a single Campaign or Organizing move. Replace the rolled stat with +[Empathy] when you trigger it. You can choose this multiple times, but it must be applied to a new move each time.

I Know a Person I Can Call

Having the moral high ground is important to the success of the campaign. You can call in the religious figures of your choice to join the workers when they take any action. Roll +[Vigor]. On a 10 or higher, the figure joins in the workers' action and costs the Boss 25 Cash. On a 7–9, the religious figure joins the workers' action but only costs the Boss 5 Cash. On a 6 or less, the figures you reach out to are unavailable and cannot participate in the action but share their regrets with the team.

Have You Talked to...?
You have a wide network of contacts. You are ubiquitous at events and rallies. When the team has hit a roadblock in finding organizing committee members, recruiting them, or repairing relationships with them, this organizer has the best chance of finding the way. Roll +[Smarts]. On a 10 or higher, carry 2 forward to moves related to leaders or declare the location of the hard-to-locate leader. On a 7–9, carry 1 forward to moves related to leaders or declare the location of the leader—but the GM will offer you a hard bargain for this information. On a 6 or less, you take one Harm for the fruitless footwork you've put in.

Choose a move from any other Tendency.

Look and Background
Choose **one** from each category.

Gender & Sexuality: (choose as you feel appropriate): CIS, L, G, B, T, Q, I, ?, ___, ___, ___, ___

Preferred Pronoun:

Clothes: Business Casual, Race T-shirt, Buttoned Down, Dapper, Flexible, _____

Body: Heavy, Leggy, Skinny, Tiny, Curvy, Coltish,_____

Eyes: Distracted, Glittering, Wide-set, Squinty, Heavy-lidded,_____

Who you relate to outside of the union:
Bandmate, Priest, Barista, _____

Vehicle: Car with a Spare Tire, Minivan, Cleanish, Station Wagon, _____

SOCIAL SERVICER

When confronted by a person in distress, a worker done wrong by the Boss, or a friend in need, the social servicer tries to take an active hand in solving the problem as soon as possible. This Tendency is challenging because your Empathy may lead your actions, but by solving problems, the social servicer robs the campaign of the issues that move workers to action. You are able to build deep and meaningful ties with the workers because of your obvious commitment to their well-being. The social servicer begins play with the capacity to maintain relationships with one additional organizing committee member.

Moves
Dark Bargain
When faced with a potential failure or a bad evaluation, you may impose a Harm or Mark on another organizer and succeed. You must narratively describe how you've sold out your colleague.

Solve the Problem, Solve the World
The core of the social servicer is making friends and smoothing waves. Choose a single Campaign or Organizing move. Replace the rolled stat with +[Moxie] when you trigger it. You can choose this multiple times, but it must be applied to a new move each time.

Turn Down the Heat
Sometimes a worker has an issue in their lives that is revealed only under the pressure that the Buster puts them under. The issue may be related to the Boss or related to some other thing. You can Repair a Relationship without a roll, but you must take a Mark for the effort.

Peace Be with You
You can build consensus among the team. You've always been good at bringing people

together. You may gain +1 ongoing when you act like a facilitator. When you act like a solo, take a Mark.

Selflessness Is the Best Policy
Your commitment to the well-being of the workers gets to be known. People at the shop as well as people around the community hold you in good regard. Once per Campaign Stage, you can bolster the support. Roll +[Empathy]. On a 10 or higher, you add 10% to the support. On a 7–9, you can add 10% to support, but you must choose one:
- Carry forward a -1 on all subsequent actions during the stage.
- Trigger a Campaign Stage complication.
- Add one to the Campaign Pool.
- One leader who you hold a relationship with has a very negative reaction to working with another organizer. Why?

Choose a move from any other Tendency.

Look and Background
Choose **one** from each category.

Gender & Sexuality: (choose as you feel appropriate): CIS, L, G, B, T, Q, I, ?, ___, ___, ___, ___

Preferred Pronoun:

Clothes: Business casual, Jazz Festival T-shirt, Exotic, Finely Detailed, Loose, _____

Body: Toned, Slim, Rounded, Short, Slender, Bulky, _____

Eyes: Kind, Sparkling, Mischievous, Cat-like, Jewel-like, _____

Who you relate to outside of the union:
Dragon Boat Team Member, Yoga Teacher, Brother, Child, _____

Vehicle: Car Seats in the Back, Low on Gas, Minivan, Old Volvo, _____

DIRECT ACTION ORGANIZER

You learned what you know from Edward Abbey and John Zerzan. You led actions at law offices and chanted in the hallways. You and your friends protected old growth in tree tripods. You made and operated puppets in Chiapan street theatres. Your instinct when faced with any issues the workers tell you about is to leap into action and be creative about making the Boss take notice too.

Moves
It Worked Last Time
You have a broad library of public educational

tools and experience with flashy actions. Your confidence fuels your efforts to move things forward with urgency. You may gain +1 ongoing when you act the solo. When you act like a facilitator, take a Mark.

More Brains than Machine

You've accumulated a large amount of experience in your life. These lessons may not have all come in a classroom or at a conference table, but you know a thing or two. Choose a single Campaign or Organizing move. Replace the rolled stat with +[Smarts] when you trigger it. You can choose this multiple times, but it must be applied to a new move each time.

Face-to-Face Confrontation

Preparing leaders to take on the Union Buster is risky proposition. If the leaders come across as too aggressive, the Union Buster comes away with sympathetic goodwill. If they underperform, the Union Buster plants the seeds of uncertainty, which impacts the support. You have lots of personal experience confronting authority figures. When you or the leaders you maintain relationships with confront the Union Buster, add +[Leaders] to the move where +[Leaders] equals the number of leaders that you as a direct action organizer maintain relationships with.

Into the Wee Dark Hours

You've been up for thirty-six hours on a hunger strike to move a college administrator to disinvest in unethical businesses. What's the Harm in staying up late to catch a conversation with a leader? Once per Campaign Stage, you can shake off two Harm from any source. Erase the Harm and proceed as normal.

They of Action

When you are part of the team that takes an action, add your +[Moxie] to the roll as you lead the chants and push participants to take more risks than they thought they would. In return for this bonus, you and each organizer that you have Regard for must take a Mark. You, the other players, and the GM decide what happened in the action that Marks y'all.

Choose a move from any other Tendency.

Look and Background

Choose one from each category.

Gender & Sexuality: (choose as you feel appropriate): CIS, L, G, B, T, Q, I, ?, ___, ___, ___, ___

Preferred Pronoun:

Clothes: Business Casual, Sloppy, Anarchist Band

T-shirt, Open-backed Shirt, Reliable, _____

Body: Flexible, Stringy, Willowy, Gaunt, Fit, Ample, _____

Eyes: Calculating, Steely, Red-rimmed, Long Lashes, Beady, _____

Who you relate to outside of the union: Anarchist Activist, Socialist Worker Party Organizer, Partner, _____

Vehicle: Dirty, Packed with Flyers, Pickup, Used Hatchback, _____

Apparatchik

Many labor unions were established near the beginning of the 1900s and have endured years of external and internal pressure. You are committed to preserving the organization that decades of members built, defended, and grew. The apparatchik puts a primary focus on the health of the union. You begin play with the capacity to maintain relationships with one fewer organizing committee member.

Moves
Rising Star
Name the person within the union who has adopted you as a protégé. You can call upon

them to assist when you debrief, check in, or have a performance evaluation. Your mentor can also provide cover if you need to skip a task to heal a Harm or two.

Political Thought

Your commitment to the movement is unassailable. You know what the leadership of the union will agree to and what is out of line. When you Act Up as a hardnose, gain +1 ongoing to enact your actions for the organizing task. When you choose to act as a solo, take a Mark.

The Union Way

You've been invited to all of the trainings that the international union hosts. You've taught some of the classes that the local has hosted for other members of the central labor council in town. Choose a single Campaign or Organizing move. Replace the rolled stat with +[Skill] when you trigger it. You may choose this multiple times but must apply it to a new move each time.

Shit Talking

Call out another organizer at the debrief and roll +[Regard]. On a 10 or higher hold three; 7–9 hold one. Spend holds one for one to give this Organizer a -1 forward or yourself a +1 going forward during this Campaign Stage.

Favors from People within the Union
Working in the labor movement has drawbacks. Not everything that you imagine is readily available. Sure, office supplies are on hand, and you can run off a hundred copies of your flyer on white paper. But there are occasions when supplies can be hard to come by: being on the road, for example, or when you need the bullhorn for an action and it's been checked out. You have connections with people all over the local labor movement. You can get access to the materials you and the team need for your campaign, but you must take a Mark for the effort.

Choose a move from any other Tendency.

Look and Background
Choose one from each category.

Gender & Sexuality: (choose as you feel appropriate): CIS, L, G, B, T, Q, I, ?, ___, ___, ___, ___

Preferred Pronoun:
Clothes: Business Casual, Sharp, Adorable, Big & Tall, Easy to Maintain, _____

Body: Skinny, Lean, Compact, Tough, Voluptuous, Sloping Shouldered, _____

Eyes: Glasses, Calm, Sweeping Eyelashes, Sunken, Deep-set, _____

Who you relate to outside of the union: Organizer Working at Another Union, Mother, No One, Your Sister, Your Brother

Vehicle: Union Made, Sedan, Hatchback, _____

POLITICAL ORGANIZER

After each election cycle, you and your colleagues poke around for some employment. After the last election, you got on at the union. You know how to identify constituents and motivate them to vote. Workers who face a contest to win recognition have to win an election. Political organizers can deliver votes, but they don't often have the best skills at building solidarity among workers. Your focus on winning a vote can bag victories for workers, but it sometimes leaves the workers in poor shape to win a good collective bargaining agreement (a contract).

Moves
Murky Past
You guard your history carefully. Choose two things you are hiding: Ivy League school, prominent family, political connections, a strange secret, portable wealth. Define them

whenever you want. Reveal either secret to save the day (succeed at a move), make an impression (add a Regard) or ruin someone (survive a debrief or performance evaluation).

Ambition

You believe that your plans are the best path forward, and no one can dissuade you. Once per Campaign Stage, gain experience when you do something against orders that causes you to tempt fate.

Get the Numbers

You can find a helpful way to divide or unify the bargaining unit. You identify a Clique or demographic that others have overlooked. Describe it. When you Chart, you add +5% to support on a successful move. When you perform a Chart move, add +[Skill] as well.

Best of the Day

During the debrief, you want to make anything you do look good. You can describe even failures in a positive light. Roll +[Moxie] to gain favor from the organizing director. On a 10 or higher, you dodge any repercussions from failure on the task. On a 7–9 you avoid repercussions but must pick one:

- The support your work contributed to is halved due to workers not being influenced.

- You gain a negative Regard from another organizer. Narrate how that happens.
- You gain one Mark.
- Add one to the Campaign Pool.

Teflon
When faced with a challenging Housevisit or attempt at recruitment, rather than rolling for that move, you succeed. But the GM either triggers a complication in this Campaign Stage, or the GM can choose to hold a complication forward for the next GM (if you choose to rotate GM duties) to use.

Choose a move from any other Tendency.

Look and Background
Choose one from each category.

Gender & Sexuality: (choose as you feel appropriate): CIS, L, G, B, T, Q, I, ?, ___, ___, ___, ___

Preferred Pronoun:

Clothes: Business Casual, Flashy, Stiff, Boho Chic, Skinny-fit, _____

Body: Fit, Toned, Stout, Overweight, Full-figured, Hourglass, _____

Eyes: Smiling, Dull, Close-set, Bright, Large, ____

Who you relate to outside of the union:
Lobbyist, Legislative Staffer, [Sports]ball
Teammate, _____

Vehicle: Saab, Audi, Volvo, Subaru, _____

ROLES

Each player will choose one of the following
roles. They can be swapped around between
Campaign Stages or kept the same. Each organizer has a part to play in the story of the
workers' victory. You may not have enough
players to fulfill each role, and that is okay.
Frequently, depending on the campaign and
industry, there may not even be six organizers
on each campaign.

- **Lead:** You Recruit well. When the Campaign Stage moves forward, take an
  Experience if none of the organizers
  ended the stage stressed.

- **Data Support:** You are awesome at
  Review the Numbers. When the Campaign
  Stage moves forward, take one Experience
  if the Primerx spoke out at an action.

- **Field Organizer:** You can Housevisit

really well. When the Campaign Stage moves forward, take one Experience if you pushed the union into taking an action it was hesitant to take.

- **Communications:** You Craft the Message unlike any other organizer. When the Campaign Stage moves forward, take one Experience if you showed a fellow organizer an error during the debrief.

- **Research Organizer:** Your insight into the Plan of Action is superior. When the Campaign Stage moves forward, take one Experience if you shared a predicted outcome and it came to pass.
- **Community Liaison:** You do an excellent job pulling everyone together to Take an Action. When the Campaign Stage moves forward, take one Experience if you got a worker's job back.

CHAPTER 3
Character Development

REGARD

Regard represents the deep feelings that can develop between two organizers. Regard can be positive or negative. In game rules, you have a +1 ongoing for any move directed toward another character (player character or nonplayer character).

At the start of the game, organizers have not built any relationships with any team members. Through the course of the campaign, organizers will build Regard for their fellow workers—love, respect, hatred, resentment, or something else. Players are encouraged to apply any flavor or type of Regard they feel best represents the narrative they have built.

There are four slots for Regard, which means there is a hard limit on the number of people that an organizer can have Regard for during the course of any campaign.

Bonus: As written above, Regard is a +1 ongoing to any moves that apply to an organizer a character has Regard for. It cannot stack. No matter how highly your colleague is respected, it will always be a +1.

Changing Regard: After you've come to Regard an organizer a certain way, you may feel it's appropriate to shift the definition of that Regard. You can shift that flavor however you want, and you can change the target between sessions or as the result of the Check In move.

There is a downside to building relationships though. If a person you have Regard for burns out and quits, regardless of your positive or negative connections you take 1 Harm right away.

Marks

Every organizer is moved and changed during their time interacting with workers. The struggle to balance the influence of capitalism is fraught with emotion and scars the hardiest of social justice warriors. It all builds toward an inevitable break in the psyche of the organizer.

A character can be Marked as the result of Tendency moves or general moves—sometimes voluntarily and sometimes not. Each Mark adds up to indelible scars, and bad things can happen to organizers when milestones in the campaign are reached.

Marks affect each Tendency differently. Sometimes a Mark can be a learning experience. Each time your character is Marked, check a box on the playbook and weave it into the narrative.

Workers, fellow organizers, and Bosses can be Marked, and that is usually their curtain call. The current GM gets to choose when the NPC leaves the story—maybe immediately or maybe down the road.

Pulling the Trigger on a Mark: The effect of a Mark can impact the game immediately, or a player can hold it until an appropriately dramatic moment to land its effect. Players may elect to reveal their Mark through a flashback too.

It may be appropriate to reveal the new Mark to people that the organizer relates to outside of work. However the Mark is implemented, the GM should find ways to plug that new Mark back into the narrative you are telling together.

The next GM should also be aware of how the Mark could impact the Campaign Stage that runs next.

Stories and Their Context: Many of the Marks indicate that something happens to the organizer, which will be the nugget of a dramatic story. When you take that Mark, the player has a few options. They can immediately relate the story and its impact on the organizer and the campaign. The players may roleplay the whole scene with organizers adopting other roles. Or the story may happen via flashback, or it could be told in some future where the outcome of the campaign is uncertain. What happened in the story? Is the organizer a reliable narrator? The player is tasked with recounting the event that Marked them, but how you all tell your story is up to you.

When to Gain a Mark: The emotion of the struggle is enough to Mark any organizer.

Choose a Mark when directed by a move or the GM.
General Marks
- Suffer the loss of a friend or lover.
- Make a friend (worker).
- Share a pitiful truth about yourself.

- Gain Experience and grow.
- Tell a class war story.
- Tell a story of home.
- Embrace burnout and face your destiny.
- Take a new Regard with an organizer.

Tendency Marks
Available only to the tendencies below.

Labor Organizer
- Put duty to worker ahead of health or love.
- Gain an obsession.
- Betray a relation or someone you have Regard for.
- Reveal a new personality quirk.

Community Organizer
- Tell a self-aggrandizing lie.
- Speak truth to power.
- Put nonlocal organizing before union organizing.
- Make a meal for the team.

Social Servicer
- Burn your relationship with a fellow worker.
- Reveal a regret.
- Adopt a pet.
- Publicly denounce a worker.

Direct Action Organizer
- Gain a bad habit that you keep a secret.
- Spread a malicious rumor.
- Ignore a problem until it overwhelms.
- Put duty to workers above health or love.

Apparatchik
- Do something against your self-interest.
- Make a bet about the outcome of a task, and make it publicly.
- Earn something you don't deserve.
- Claim something as your own.

Political Organizer
- Acquire a dread or superstition.
- Call dangerous attention to yourself.
- Tell the unvarnished truth.
- Abandon a comrade.

HARM

One Harm means that you are tired after long days at work.

Two Harm means that the grueling schedule of the campaign has stressed you out.

Three Harm means that all of that stress has lowered your immune system and you've caught a cold. This may knock you out of action for a couple days. Depending on the part of the campaign and the relationships you hold with workers, that may be a crucial time to be sick.

Four Harm means that you have finally burned out and you need to step away from the campaign for a while.

When the Campaign Stage moves forward, all lingering Harm is reduced by one. Victories, even minor ones, can lift organizers' spirits.

WAYS TO HEAL HARM

- For 1 Harm, get some rest or a couple of beers. A fellow organizer could also Check In and choose that as a result of a good roll.
- For 2 Harm, skip a task, and rest.
- For 3 harm, go to the doctor, and bring a note in from them.

CAMPAIGN POOL

The game starts with one point in the Campaign Pool for each player, including the GM.

This is a shared resource generated by actions that organizers take. It represents the power of camaraderie, preparation, momentum, and fighting spirit. A highly stacked pool represents a smoothly running group of organizers with high spirits and good cheer. All things are running well. A group acting with a low pool represents the frustrations and infighting that sadly happen too often during the length of a campaign.

This Campaign Pool is a communal resource represented by tokens. Each can be traded to the GM for +1 forward during the Organizing Stage of the campaign. Any organizer can take a token from the pool to help with any roll as long as organizers are out in the field.

Organizers can spend as many points at once as needed. It may mean others will not have this resource when they run into trouble on a Housevisit, but if some organizer feels they need a success, they totally can do it.

You can spend from the pool before or after a roll.

Unspent tokens are lost at the end of the current Organizing Stage.

Ways to Earn Campaign Pool

- Act Up and choose adding to the Pool as an outcome.
- Check In and choose to add to the Campaign Pool.
- If playing the political organizer and making the Best of the Day move, choose to add to the Campaign Pool.
- When performing the move Chart, choose to add to the Campaign Pool.
- If playing the social servicer and making the Selflessness Is the Best Policy move, choose to add to the Campaign Pool.

EXPERIENCE

When you gain Experience as an organizer, you gain new tools for talking to workers, you master a new technique, or in some other way you get to be a better organizer.

Several tasks at each Stage will include Experience for anyone who participates. When you advance the campaign to its next stage, if you meet the condition of your role, you will also gain Experience.

When you earn Experience you can choose from four options. You may choose these options more than once.

- **Harsh Lessons:** You may choose a new move. You have some that are specific to your Tendency and the option to take one from another Tendency.
- **Deepening Ties:** You can open a Regard slot and fill it in. Once you have opened a Regard slot, you can change its tone at will and the comrade it points at between sessions or by Checking In. This advance can be taken a number of times.
- **Personal Growth:** Through action and reflection, you may raise Skill, Smarts, Vigor, Empathy, or Moxie by one, up to a maximum of +3.
- **Added Responsibility:** Due to performance in the field, you gain access to added duties. For each campaign

book, there will be a chart limiting the number of leader relationships that each organizer can maintain. Relationships take time and energy to keep viable. As you gain more experience, you'll learn new ways to keep those relationships alive. You will be able to add one to the campaign's limited number of leader relationships. This Experience can be taken more than once.

WHEN THE EXPERIENCE ENDS

If you run out of options (you have raised all stats to +3 and gained all the moves for your tendency and you've built regards with each organizer) to your Experience before the workers ratify their contract, a couple of things can happen:

- Your character is too valuable to the union and is hired by the international union to run projects related to the industry that you and your fellow organizers are working with. Make up a new organizer.
- Every time you earn Experience, instead lower a stat by one, erase a move, or close a Regard slot as your character slides toward Burnout.

Ways to Earn Experience

- Trigger a move that includes Experience.
- Choose a Mark that includes Experience.
- Complete a task that triggers Experience.
- Change Campaign Stages after fulfilling your role or Tendency's condition.

CHAPTER 4
The Dice Mechanic

When a move asks that you roll dice, you will roll two six-sided dice and add the results together, along with the +[Stat] noted in the description of the move. If you have any Regard for the subject of the move, you will add +1 to the roll.

If your organizer earns "+1 forward," that means she adds one to her next relevant roll. It is a bonus that is used only once. It may be conditional, situational, or time-limited. There is one exception to this rule: the roleplaying bonus elected by the players during a Recruit or Housevisit move. If the players feel that the performance warrants an additional bonus, it can stack on top of other bonuses.

If your organizer earns a hold, that is a bonus you can use now or in the future—whenever you feel it makes sense. Holds do not stack, so you can't apply three of them at once.

If the result is a ten or more (noted as 10+), your organizer will succeed at the test with no hassles.

If the result is a six or less (noted as 6-), you are not going to succeed, and it may really suck for you. The GM will make sure that you don't like the outcome. You have handed the GM a golden opportunity to drive things into the ditch.

The most dramatic and narratively exciting results lie between seven and nine (noted as 7-9). These three numbers mean that you succeed (yay) but at a cost (boo). The GM will offer you some bargain, or you will be able to propose your own result. For most moves, there will be a few options to get your mind going in the right direction and give a sense for the scale of hardship.

Each player will have an opportunity to perform moves that abstractly reflect their efforts for the day. Organizers can do two moves each campaign day. These moves can be in any combination of Organizing, Campaign, or Tendency. In the course of a week, any one organizer can perform 10 to 14 tasks (14 if the organizers choose to work weekends). There are time limitations on every campaign, either because of union resources or some legal framework. Organizers will need to be mindful of how they spend their time under these pressures. Days lost to getting the best results or sickness have a cost.

There are two types of actions players can take: inward-facing actions (Campaign moves) and outward-facing actions (Organizing moves). The work of organizers consists of digesting large concepts—such as macroeconomics, microaggressions, class war, etc.—into viscerally understandable terms for every worker. When doing outward-facing work, an organizer may be more guarded in their choice of words than when they are kicking around the office. Words have impact, and a good organizer needs to know who is in their audience.

The Boss (played by the GM) is also able to make one move per day if they are aware that a campaign is happening.

Campaign Moves

These moves reflect the things that organizers do to prepare for their work in the field.

Moves
Check In

When you assess the state of a person or situation, roll +[Empathy]. On a 10+, choose two; on a 7–9 choose one. Spend those options now or later to ask a question. Take +1 forward when you act on the answers, or give +1 forward to another and share in the outcome if you prefer. Ask:

- How can I help out?
- What does the organizer want?
- What am I overlooking?
- How can I get...?
- If you have Regard for an organizer, you can also opt for one of the below:
- Remove one Harm each from yourself and your friend.
- Change the target and/or flavor of a currently filled Regard slot.
- Add one to the Campaign Pool.

On a miss, the GM might offer a straight-up lie, a misunderstanding, an honest mistake, or a blend of these.

A Check In has two uses: first, to aid an organizer in need; and second, to get help in understanding a difficult situation. If you need something, Check In before you try to get it. The Check In can be a form of intimacy. It's fine to reach out to relations outside of the union too.

Plan an Action

In the office, prior to marching on the Boss or delivering a petition, an organizer will need to assess the merits of the action. Who will the audience be? What is downside of failing/what is the result of success? How much energy will organizers need to put into the action for it to work well? Who is the target of the action? To determine what it looks like to answer these questions, roll +[Smarts]. On a 10+, you hold +1 on Take an Action following your plan. On a 7–9, the GM will offer you two hard bargains about the assumptions you've made. (The researcher of the group only has to choose one of the options the GM offers.) On a 6-, you have grossly overestimated the result of the action; carry a -1 forward to Take an Action following your plan.

Tempt Fate
When you Tempt Fate, you roll +[Moxie]. On a 10+, you succeed on getting your action advanced. On a 7–9, you do it but not without a hard choice. The GM can offer you a worse outcome, a hard bargain, or an ugly choice. On a 6-, you take harm and are Marked in addition to failing.

Tempt Fate is the default move for any harebrained situation an organizer may find themselves in while away from the field. Trying to Identify the Primerx won't Tempt Fate, but deliberately challenging the Organizing Director about the task assignments for the day will.

Craft the Message
Once organizers have identified a campaign issue, they should take time to think about how to relate these sometimes complex or abstract issues to the wider world. A good message connects with the key constituents affected by any issue. A great message is universally understood.

Organizers should identify the audience that needs to be reached by the message (impacted people, allies, and the target). This message should grow from a clear vision of the solution and convey a concrete demand. The players should workshop whatever message they wish to use on this campaign. Roll +[Skill]. On a 10+, the message crafted is great and communicates all of the information you need it to. You may carry +1 forward to Flyer or Plan an Action. On a 7–9, choose two (communicators choose one):

- The message doesn't resonate with one part of the audience. Which one?
- The message is not concrete enough. It's too wordy, unclear, or something else.
- The message is tactically good but will create a complication with your overall strategy.
- The message does not inspire the emotions you anticipated. What happens?
- The solution you identified is unwinnable: too big, too small, or wrong?

Review the Numbers
This move represents all of the time organizers spend staring at lists of assessed workers or stacks of data looking for patterns and discerning their secrets. When you Review the Numbers, roll +[Smarts]. On a 10+:

- Identify the Biggest Worst (the largest

section of workers with the least support) or the Primerx or another leader (organizer's choice), or

- you gather all up the relevant facts about an employer or Decision Maker (Cash on hand, Public Capital, business expenses, business-related income, etc.).

On a 7–9, you identify a Clique (all of the staring at the wall pays off: add 5% to your majority), the Biggest Worst, a Leader, the Primerx, or data on the Boss—but not without consequence. The researcher chooses one:

- It's not the Primerx: your work identifies the wrong Leader as a Primerx.
- The Biggest Worst is stone cold to any attempts at organizing.
- The Clique's Leader is difficult to Recruit. Hold -1 forward on attempts to Recruit that Leader.
- Your total count is wrong, and it costs the team 10% Support.
- The Leader's influence doesn't cover as many people as you thought.
- The data is incorrect in a small way (+ or -20%).
- Identify the wrong Decision Maker. Who is really in charge here? Carry a -1 forward to Plan an Action.
- You overlook a key lever to motivate the decision maker. What one? Carry a -1

forward to Plan an Action.
- You overlook an important ally of the Decision Maker. Who? Carry a -1 forward to Plan an Action.

On a 6-, you find no information today, or you have identified the wrong Decision Maker. When you Take an Action, you and your activists find yourself in the wrong place.

Act Up

Acting Up means behaving in an uncooperative manner. A solo believes that the only way to get something done right is for you to accomplish a task by yourself. A hardnose is immovable and uncompromising in ensuring their vision moves forward. Facilitators force people to compromise on their positions and settle on an action. When you try to get your way:
- by acting like a hardnose, roll +[Moxie].
- by acting like a solo roll, +[Vigor].
- by acting like a facilitator, roll +[Empathy]

On a 10+, choose two; on a 7–9, choose one:
- Make someone do what you want. (If the person you are imposing on is another organizer, they can do it or not, but if they don't, you'll both be Marked.)
- Add one to the Campaign Pool.
- Make sure there will be no repercussions from your outburst.

On a miss, there will be trouble.

Organizing Moves

These moves represent all of the outward-facing work that organizers do.

Moves
Housevisit

Go out and find a worker at home. Roll +[Skill]. On a 10+, your conversation moves the worker to take the action, whatever it may be—signing a card, identifying a leader, or marching on the Boss. On a 7–9, you move them to act, but you choose two consequences (field organizers choose one):

- Everyone in the Housevisit takes a Mark.
- Your supporter talks at work. Your visit has triggered a Boss action.
- An organizer in your team takes Harm. GM's choice.
- The recruitment effort has a flaw, and it's your fault.

On a 6-, the worker is not home or is not interested in what you have to say. Or you can press on and Tempt Fate (Organizers each choose one).

Flyer

Roll +[Vigor]. On a 10+, your flyering recruits a worker. On a 7–9, you recruit the worker, but you choose two consequences:

- The recruitment effort has a flaw, and it's your fault.

- Bring a -1 forward to take an action in this Campaign Stage.
- Take a Mark or give a Mark to another organizer.
- Trigger a Boss move.
- The flyer pushes worker buttons in the wrong way: lose 2 or 2% Support.

On a 6-, all organizers participating in the Flyer action take a Harm.

Before You Roll the Dice

Good roleplay (as judged by the other organizers) can gain up to a +3 on a roll or add one to the Campaign pool.

Note on Raps: Each organization and each campaign will have their own Rap, a script, that organizers use to move workers through a conversation. A written Rap is not within the scope of this game. Each union local or each roleplaying group can use whatever methods they wish to prepare for and execute their Housevisits.

Tempt Fate

When you Tempt Fate, you roll +[Moxie]. On a 10+, you succeed at what you are trying to do. On a 7–9, you do it but are forced to make a hard choice. The GM can offer you a worse outcome, a hard bargain, or an ugly choice.

On a 6-, you take Harm as established and are Marked in addition to failing.

Recruit

Roll +[Skill]. On a 10+, you get the worker you need actively on board. On a 7–9, you get the worker on board, but you choose two consequences (Lead Organizers choose one):

- The Leader has a fatal hesitation that will reveal itself when the GM chooses. The Leader will flip later in the campaign.
- They agree to be on board, but the first time they are tested, they hesitate to act.
- The first organizer who Recruits this leader is the only organizer that Leader will talk to.
- The Leader wants a specific thing done in the Negotiations or Resolution Stage and is adamant they heard the organizer promise it would happen.
- Take a Mark.
- The Leader connects with and moves half the normal amount of activists.

On a 6- you fail to Recruit this Leader. The door is not closed to reapproaching this worker.

Repair Relationship

Roll +[Empathy]. On a 10+, you get the worker back actively on board. On a 7–9, you get the worker on board, but you choose two consequences (community organizers choose one.)

- The worker will follow through but not immediately.

- You don't get the worker on board in the approved manner. What did you do?
- The worker reveals a quirk in their lives that now must be managed going forward.

On a 6-, you send the worker back to their shift still unconfirmed. Maybe that is obvious, and maybe it is not. Regardless, one Harm from the effort is likely.

Workers changing their minds during the course of an organizing drive is a fact of life. The Boss can make being certain that a union is the right solution to their problems hard. The Boss's campaign is based on sowing doubt or uncertainty and raising the level of stress on the job. Organizers have to be in constant contact with workers throughout every stage of a campaign.

Take an Action

This move covers all the various actions that can be taken during the course of a campaign: deliver a petition, picket, street theater. Use Take an Action to determine the outcome. Roll +[Vigor]. On a 10+, add 6 or 6% to the workers' support. On a 7–9, your action succeeds (add 6 or 6% support), and you choose two consequences (community organizers choose one):

- Your action pushes the wrong buttons, and the workers don't support it. Lose 5 or 5% support.

- Costs the Boss 25 Cash/PC in bad public relations.
- All organizers taking part in the action take a Harm.
- The organizer who planned the action has to answer for something that went wrong during the Debrief. Describe what happened wrong.
- Add one to the Campaign Pool.
- The workers' action violates the law. That is something that may have long-term implications for the strength of the workers' union.
- The action is half effective (3 or 3% support).
- The Decision Maker agrees to the demand, but a plan for implementation is never agreed to.
- The Decision Maker agrees to meet but is noncommittal about when.

On a 6-, the Boss or Decision Maker does not meet with the leaders (hides, flees, or locks the doors). Relations with 2d6 Leaders are Harmed and will need repairing. Reduce Harm by half if Leaders were inoculated to this possibility.

Special Moves

Moves
Debrief
Once a week, Organizers meet with the Organizing Director and Debrief the week's work. When you Debrief, tell the Organizing Director what went well and what went wrong. If the Task was unusually stressful, the GM may add one Harm. If you wish, change the tone of an existing Regard. If you are an apparatchik, publicly shame a fellow organizer and add one to the next day's Campaign Pool. If it was the Campaign Stage's last Task, begin Next Steps.

If you Tempted Fate or something went wrong with your Task, be prepared to face any consequences. You may have to participate in a Performance Evaluation.

Briefing
When campaign day starts, consult with the GM and inform the organizers about the coming objectives. Players should choose and check off a Task from the Campaign Stage sheet and announce it to the organizers.

All player characters should participate. They can choose their moves based on the Campaign Stage needs and depending on the Task. If the organizer opts to heal a Harm and shirks a Task, they can answer for that in the Debrief.

Performance Evaluation
If you are evaluated by the Organizing Director, roll +[Moxie] if you lie or +[Smarts] if you tell the truth. On a 10+, they thank you for your work. On a 7–9, choose one:

- You and the fellow organizer of your choice are Marked.
- You slag a fellow organizer and throw them under the bus for the outcome of a Task.
- You agree to keep an eye on a fellow organizer.

Buster Confrontation
You may encounter a Union Buster. Every employer hires a Union Buster. They advertise themselves as helping to keep employers union-free. Busters are trained lawyers being paid hundreds of dollars per billable hour to sow doubt about workers' collective strength. They are slick. They lurk around the workplace intimidating workers and implying outcomes to things they do not know.

If you Track the Buster to learn what he's saying, roll +[Vigor]. On a 10+, you may hold +1 for Flyering, or the next Boss move is half as effective in eroding your support (improved Inoculation). On a 7–9, you improve your

Flyering or you Inoculate the workers well (Boss move is half as effective) and you must choose one:

- You and any other organizer who is tagging along take a harm.
- The next Boss move is slightly more effective—the message changes. Increase the support lost by 5 or 5%.
- A Leader's relationship with another organizer is damaged because the Buster catches on to the leak and increases the pressure on a worker.

On a 6-, your effort to follow the Buster backfires. The Buster now has your identity, and it will be used by the GM.

If you Confront the Buster with workers around, roll +[Smarts]. On a 10+, you add 10 or 10% to support. On a 7–9, you add 10 or 10% to support, but you must choose an outcome:

- The Boss moves target the acting organizer. They are called out as part of the Boss Campaign (see below) by name as a troublemaker. Their relationships with their Leaders are damaged.
- You must take a mark.
- GM may initiate a Boss move immediately.

On a 6-, your confrontation is off-putting, and the Buster comes out on top. Lose 10 or 10% support.

If you monkey wrench that Buster's day-to-day schedule, roll +[Moxie]. On a 10+, you increase the cost of all the Boss Moves in this Campaign Stage by 25%. On a 7–9, you increase the costs of all the Boss moves in this Campaign Stage by 25%, but you must choose one.

- You and all the organizers who participate are Marked by the effort.
- The police are called on you. Miss all Tasks from next 2d6 days of this Campaign Stage as you deal with that.
- Relations with one organizer's Leaders are damaged. GM's choice of who is affected.

On a 6-, your shenanigans do not impact the Buster in the least. Maybe you got the hotel room number wrong. Take a Harm for the efforts.

Next Steps

When all Tasks have been completed and/or the organizers feel that you're ready to move on, advance to the next Campaign Stage. Each campaign has distinct stages that mark progress. Refer to the campaign playbooks to gain insight into conditions that are the most advantageous. Capitalism will only relinquish what it is made to, and the march of justice surges on.

Any player can change the Campaign Stage but I suggest you consult with everyone before you do. When a player chooses this, the entire Campaign moves forward toward the resolution that the workers desire. This move has the following additional effects:

- Anyone who fulfilled their Role conditions can get Experience.
- Anyone can change their Role if they wish, including rotating the role of GM.
- The GM should orient everyone to the new Campaign Stage and continue.

If you are at Ratification Stage and choose this move, celebrate the workers' victory in improving their lives.

QUITTING

Turnover among organizers is common. Organizing workers can be a thankless job, and it can contain lots of stress. It may be common for organizers in the game to not make it through a whole campaign from first contact to ratification.

Four Harm leads to the final Burnout. Harm stacks in this game, meaning sickness striking a stressed-out organizer could spell their end.

One of the Marks also leads to Quitting. Any organizer can choose to take it if it's the best of all the bad options. Eventually, Embrace Burnout will be the only Mark left to you, and from there it is a short trip to your last day on the campaign.

If your character quits, consider assuming the GM role for a while. When it fits the narrative and feels right, you can assume the role of an NPC who has already been introduced, or you can introduce an entirely new organizer— green, idealistic, and fresh from college.

Boss Moves

These special moves are outlined in each Campaign Stage and is relevant to the type of campaign playbook you are running. Bosses don't roll dice. They spend money. The moves that the GM gets to unleash during each stage are based on how much Cash or Public Capital (PC) the Boss has on hand. The Boss spends however much they would like to perform their moves in each Campaign Stage. The Boss's moves simply succeed if they've spent enough money on them.

Each stage refreshes an amount Cash or Public Capital determined by the campaign stage. Public Capital refers to the good will Decision Makers spend while they are targets of an issue focused organizing campaign. Cash is the Boss resource for union organizing drives. The Boss takes their moves last each Campaign day.

Organizers should share in advance what tactics the Boss is likely to use (which organizers call "inoculating") with the leaders they recruit and the workers that they Housevisit. If they inoculate, then the Boss move is half as effective at its goals of eroding support or damaging relationships.

CHAPTER 5
The Game Master

Everyone could have an opportunity to fill the role of the Game Master, or GM, but the game would be best run by someone who has a good sense of an organizing campaign. Novice organizers may gain a new understanding of what goes into an organizing drive should they take on the role of the GM. Decide amongst yourselves who should GM the beginning game. The role of GM can fluidly move around the group based on Burnout or a change in the Campaign Stage.

  The GM plays the part of the Boss and the Organizing Director. They breathe life into the rest of the world around the organizers. The GM establishes the basics of the union local. The starting GM gets the opportunity to name and characterize the important faces, like the president of the local, the lawyer, and the Boss. The GM sets creative obstacles in the path of the workers who are trying to organize and also makes real how hard it is to motivate workers to overcome their fear of upsetting the order of their universe.

Everyone in the group should have a character ready to play, including the starting GM if the role is to be passed around. The initial GM's character can hang around the office or come to the party late after the first contact is made. Everyone will help the GM out by playing the part of the workers who are moved to act through good roleplay or hesitate to join because the organizer never connected with their key issue.

Everyone should be familiar with the GM's List of Four (see below). They set the tone and open the way for lots of story hooks.

The GM never rolls dice.

While the GM has a lot on their plate, it isn't their sole responsibility to organize these workers or tell a story about it. The players have the responsibility to be creative and think through the solution to the workers' challenges. Organizers are there to help workers make the right decisions to overcome the resistance of their Bosses.

The best advice for making the nonplayer

characters, or NPCs, relevant is to drive their wants and needs directly at the players. During every Organizing move, the organizing committee wants something from the organizers, or during each Campaign move, the Organizing Director has some feedback on the plan.

Things in a campaign can go really well, or they can go stupendously bad. Workers can have great depths of solidarity, or the Boss can fire everyone. Any outcome has organizing potential. Embrace the failure and unpredictability of the dice. Players want to win. Capitalism is the theft of value from the labor of the workers, after all, and is a sickness to human relationships. But complications in the fight for justice are common. As GM, you get to wield hardship in the service of learning and narrative.

THE LIST OF FOUR

- **Agenda:** This is more than getting ready for a meeting. Your agenda is a list of GM goals. Every curveball you throw to the players should serve your agenda. This is the struggle for organizers to lead a group of leaders to equity and fairness.

- **Principles:** Use these techniques to drive your agenda.

- **Moves:** As a GM you get way more flexibility than a player organizer. Your moves can be as hard as you like. You may feel that Bosses have a good heart and their tactics are all about allowing everyone to keep having a job. Remember: Bosses make a living off of other people's work. Let the events play out, and the dice can direct fate.

- **Threats:** These are everything about organizing that challenges the players: rent, heartbreak, fear, hate, and paperwork. Each Threat has a move. Choose a Threat or three for each Campaign Stage. As GM, it's your place to set the tone for organizing.

AGENDA

Bring it to life: Each Campaign Stage has details. Every hotel the organizers stay in is different in subtle ways. Draw the details out to reinforce the color of your world.

Put them in the trenches: Once a campaign starts, it can be a dramatic series of emotional meetings that drag late into the night and start early in the morning. Organizers work the same schedule as workers: 6:00 a.m. shift changes with an hour-and-a-half bus ride. There's too much to do in twenty-four hours.

Seek out their stories: Plug every leading statement and every emotion back into the narrative for your characters.

Play to find out how the workers won: Do not assume you know how the workers are going to pull this one out. Be interested in what the organizers bring to the planning and execution of the game.

Principles

Let things start and end in the fiction: Let the story the players share direct the action of the workers' campaign. Just see what develops and keep asking, "What happens next?"

Address the organizers: Your organizers are more fictionalized versions of the players. Players can make fiction versions of themselves, or they can try on the outlandish costumes of a person of opposite type. When you are asking how the flyer looks or debriefing the organizers, don't ask the player, ask the organizer. It may seem insignificant, but it aids the immersion.

Point the action at the organizers: All of the narrative for how the workers' succeed at getting fairness out of an inherently unfair economic system should relate directly to the events in the hotel, or at the jobsite, or in the homes of the worker. Getting hung up on SCOTUS decisions, or federal or state legislation, is a distraction from the drama of workers taking action. That high-level thinking obscures the truth that the economy is rigged against worker justice.

Flesh out the NPCs: Make the Boss, the Leaders, the workers, and the Organizing Director interesting. Give them goals and hesitations. But don't dote on these characters; they aren't precious. NPCs should serve the purpose of the story, and the invisible hand of the market isn't kind to laborers.

Sometimes just give it to the players: It is certainly fine, in the aims of mixing up the tempo of the Campaign, to occasionally say to the group, "Everything today went smoothly. What do you do?"

GM Moves

Let these things happen as part of the unfolding story. One does not simply say, "Inflict Harm." Narrate the impending action that will stress the organizer. Ask how long the Primerx talked to them about unrelated things. Ask how many workers in the parking lot blew past them while they stood in the heat and held limp flyers.

Soft Moves

This is a chance for you to ask more questions. They should be loaded with meaning and results that move the events of the Campaign forward. Soft moves reflect an option for the GM to allow the organizers to move forward without fully punishing a failure. Make a soft move when a hard move is too harsh.

Make a soft move to foreshadow the impending moves. When players wait for you to fill in the details of the story, make sure the Boss comes out ahead.

Tiring an organizer is an easy soft move.

The Anti Committee
As the organizers set out to create and lead an organizing committee in the community to at the workplace the Boss is setting out to create or re-initiate their own committee of anti-union workers. It may be a race to recruit the natural leaders. The Boss can move messages that may be illegal for them to voice through a committee like this.

Hard Moves

Is it a good time to illustrate exactly how hard a Boss can be? Yes, it is. Break out the hard stuff. The Campaign has lots of hard events that try the will of organizers.

Make a hard move when someone fails a roll (6-). Make a hard move if the organizers delay action on a shitty thing happening at the shop. Make a hard move when it makes sense in the narrative flow of the game.

You should respect momentum, though, when organizers are doing well. When organizers are doing the bulk of the work moving the narrative forward and fleshing out their own antagonists, let them carry on without GM meddling.

THREATS

Statistically this type of dice system results in lots of success with a choice of complications. Moves will compound and create more opportunities for conflict. Part of being a successful organizer is taking what on first glance could be a setback and using it to launch a menu of new steps forward. A stubborn, one-dimensional organizer quickly burns out.

Failure at any move should be as interesting as success. Overcoming these obstacles is what makes organizing a constantly engaging endeavor. As a GM, you should always end the description of the failure with, "What do you do?"

Broadly, the moves a GM should inject into the game follow these examples.

- Show them darkness on the horizon. Telegraph that the shit storm is on its way.
- Bring a threat to bear. Pay off the results of the brewing storm.
- Reveal an unwelcome truth about the worker, the Boss, or the union. Lay down

a fact that all organizers wish were not true. There are things in each organizing campaign that can curdle the innards of the hardest class warrior: The Boss is selling the company. The worker is respected by her coworkers, but they also fear her. The local president is having an affair.

- Turn their move back on them. Whatever benefits a move has given the organizer can have a negative impact as well. Convincing the Primerx to come on board may result in her enemy joining the Anti Committee.

- Give an opportunity that suits their Tendency. Each Tendency of the organizer has a strength and a habit that isn't necessarily helpful. The labor organizer knows how it's done. The social servicer is empathetic. Make a move that fits the Tendency's strength.

- Explore the flip side of every organizer's strength. The labor organizer can get stuck in a rut. The social servicer inhibits stoking the raging fire that workers must touch in order to overcome their fears.

- Inflict Harm. In non-game terms, you can lay some serious damage to the status quo in each Campaign Stage.

- Offer an opportunity and make it cost

something. Make the opportunities impossibly tempting and the cost equally high. Any move that brings a possible Experience is a good place to lay down a real bargain.

- Put them somewhere they don't want to be: between the Boss and the Primerx, between the Primerx and their coworkers, between the Organizing Director and the Organizing Committee (OC). Take any opportunity for the GM to drive the drama forward.

- After every move ask, "What do you do now?" This simple question keeps the organizer up at night when the worker is hiding from you or when the Boss hires the Buster.

These are more concrete ways that threats can be brought to bear on the organizers.

The "No Match" Letter (per the Justice Department Website) is a written notice issued by the Social Security Administration (SSA) to an employer, usually in response to an employee wage report, advising that the name or Social Security number (SSN) reported by the employer for one or more employees does not "match" a name or SSN combination reflected in SSA's records. The difference between Bob, Rob, and Robert will also trigger one of these letters. These letters are frequently used to intimidate immigrant workers.

The Boss
- The Anti Committee moves a vote no petition.
- Message: the union is a third party.
- Message: your signature is important; don't sign anything.
- Message: don't talk about what you get paid.
- Mandatory meetings that all staff attend and hear about how dumb a union is.
- Letters nearly threatening workers' jobs or the "No Match" letter from ICE.

The Union
- Lawsuit filed against the local unrelated to the campaign.
- Lawsuit filed against another local unrelated to any campaign.
- Lawsuit filed against another union in town.
- Bad union experience.
- Election for officers.
- Election for politician.
- Officers want to share the shine from victorious workers.

The Team
- Petty squabbles, spread rumors and gossip.
- Confess love.

- Celebrate victory.
- Mourn the lost.
- Deliver bad news from outside the union, or someone an organizer relates to has bad news.
- Take credit.
- Borrow resources or equipment.
- Break the rules and get away with it.

Internal Organizers
- A different department manager runs the debrief.
- Other tasks as assigned could take you away from the field.
- Help with membership actions.

Legal
- Unfair Labor Practice needs to be filed
- Unit clarification hearing.
- Supreme Court case about union.

The Press
- Bad news from the state.
- Bad op-ed about union goals.
- Bad press about the campaign.

Outside Influence
- Holidays
- Weather (snowstorm, etc.)

Each type of campaign (skilled nursing, acute care, community issue, manufacturing, etc.) and each Campaign Stage has its own threat options. These options will be included in each playbook.

CHAPTER 6
Playing the Game

CHOOSE A GM

To begin playing, someone will need to volunteer to be the first GM. You picked up the book, so guess what—you are it. For information about the finer points of what you will be doing to dramatically torture the players, go to chapter 5 for moves and principles.

Throughout the game, players advance the Campaign through different Stages, and at each one the GM role can change hands. In a union setting, organizers have varying levels of skill and experience. Less experienced organizers can gain insight about the goals and focus of a union or a Boss by operating in the role of the GM. Your group can come to terms with the role of the GM. As the RPG Academy puts it, "If you're having fun, you're doing it right."

While you are acting as GM, your organizer is safe from Harm. You should establish in the narrative the reason for your character being away from the field. Why has the organizer stepped back from their role? Are they on vacation, sick, taking a Family and Medical Leave Act absence? When they return to the field, determine who GMs next.

You could assign the Stages ahead of time to each player so that section will be prepared. Then when it comes time for each person to GM, they can make it something unique and memorable.

ESTABLISH PLAYING TIME

You've gotten a group of friends together. They want to use this game for training or for entertainment or for entertaining training. Discuss how long they want to play for this session and how long they want the Campaign to last. Do they want to go from first contact through the ratification of a collective bargaining agreement? Do you?

You can totally play *Beat the Boss* as a one-night-only game. You can pick out the Stage that you and your fellow organizers are about to embark on in real life and run through that section to get prepared. While the players are making their organizers, the GM should review the Campaign Stage that you want to play. Take note of the questions and the moves involved. Focus on the most important things to dramatize. Flesh out some of the workers, Bosses, and others in the Stage and what they want from their union and from the organizers.

Based on which Campaign Stage you start at, have players choose an equal number of Marks and Experiences. Ask about these Marks and Experiences: Can you tie them into the Stage, the NPCs, and the narrative?

It's important to get everyone at the table to have similar expectations now.

MAKE CHARACTERS

Beat the Boss can be used to sharpen organizers' skills to prepare to go out and shepherd workers through their fight to build their own union, or it can be a drama-packed tabletop roleplaying game where players gain a glimpse into the work it takes to resist the thievery of capitalism.

Players can make alter egos that are unrelated to their everyday experience, or organizers can closely reflect the players themselves. Either way, organizers will have some statistics that highlight strengths and weaknesses, Roles, and a few identifying features that will set them apart.

Your players' organizers should complement and contrast with one another. A team of organizers in the field have different strengths and tendencies. The team at your table should work together to craft their organizers to be interesting during the game.

Everyone plays the role of an organizer—maybe heroic, maybe hardheaded, maybe callous, or all of these things—at different Campaign Stages.

Tendencies: It can be illuminating to choose a Tendency that is at odds with your natural instincts so that you can see through another organizer's eyes. You can also play to your own personal strengths if that is your taste. When in doubt about what to do, look to the description of your Tendency. Characters start with their choice of two moves. More can be added as the game progresses. That is what Experience is for.

Name: Choose your own or use some heroic-sounding name. People that have a Regard for you could dub you with a nickname. Let that come out in the game.

Look: Each Tendency has a few options for a number of looks. They are merely suggestions and can be interpreted as you like or replaced with any descriptive terms you imagine.

Stats: Choose your stats. For organizers starting from the beginning, you can opt to be an organizer or a senior organizer. Senior organizers can add a total of +2 to Skill, Vigor, Smarts, Empathy, and Moxie (e.g., +0, +1, -1, +2, +0 or +0, +2, +0, +0, +0). Organizers can add a total of +1 to stats. Organizers-in-training (OIT) start with a total of 0 in stats.

- **Skill** is a measure of academic training, union training, and assiduous attention to detail. It is most useful for Recruiting Primerxs and Housevisiting any worker. You must put all of the things you've learned in training to use to overcome the hesitations of the worker.
- **Vigor** is a measure of stamina, endurance, and toughness. Organizers rely on guts to last through long days of Housevisiting, standing in the parking lot or outside of the worksite Flyering, or preparing and leading a group of workers to march on the Boss.
- **Smarts** is a measure of raw talent and sharpness of mind. Smarts come in handy when you chart the workplace to look for the pattern in the assessments or when you imagine the snags and hurdles that may come to pass when Planning an Action.
- **Empathy** is a measure of an organizer's way with workers and the community. A low Empathy score leaves an organizer

cold to others' problems, while an organizer rich in Empathy connects with people easily and deeply. Workers trust an Empathetic organizer easily.

- **Moxie** is the measure of personal courage and determination in the face of social, political, or economic pressure to act otherwise. Organizers call upon Moxie to show no fear when Tempting Fate. The odds of workers organizing in modern America are ever stacked against success, and organizers will need plenty of Moxie to move the Boss.

Roles: In each team of organizers, there are some roles that are filled. The roles reflect the varied nature of the things that need to be addressed during the length of the campaign. The roles can be switched during the length of the campaign due to absence or as a skill-building opportunity. Players will fill the lead organizer, data support, field organizer, community organizer, research organizer, or communications Role at some point during the campaign.

  If you have fewer than six players, an NPC from the local will fill the roles missing from the team. That NPC will have their own needs and goals that the GM gets to establish through the narrative.

Support: For each Campaign stage after the first, organizer Tasks will count for and against the Support that the workers build toward their majority. It legally takes 50 percent plus one to win the recognition election, but workers don't win a convincingly good contract with a bare majority. The larger you can build the majority for your Support prior to the get out the vote (GOTV) effort, the more workers can win at the bargaining table.

If you are organizing a community to resolve a persistent issue that is harming them, you will be building a number of supporters rather than a percent of supporters. The more community members who stand in the office of a Decision Maker and share their stories, the more likely the correct decision will be made.

Organizers should share in advance what tactics the Boss is likely to use (known as "inoculating") with the leaders they recruit and the workers that they Housevisit. If they inoculate, then the Boss move is half as effective at its goals of eroding support or damaging relationships.

Leader Capacity: Each organizer will have a cap on how many leaders they can maintain relationships with. Sometimes this limit is based on shifts that leader works. It is unreasonable for one organizer to maintain relationships with leaders on all three shifts. The organizer would never sleep. You might want to determine the leader relationship capacity for each organizer per campaign type. This way if you have a large group playing, everyone can get some experience leading OC members.

If you are playing a campaign book for a large employee industry (e.g., manufacturing or acute care), you should scale up the cap on OC being covered by organizers.

Boss Moves: The Boss will begin each Campaign Stage with an amount of Cash or Public Capital. For example, the Skilled Nursing Home Boss starts the first Stage with 100 Cash. Cash and Public Capital are abstract ways to track the resources on hand for any Boss. As described in chapter 5, the Boss doesn't roll dice. The Boss will spend their Cash or Public Capital to erode the support that the workers have built by taking their actions. The Boss can take a move at the end of each organizing day. The GM does not need to announce the move that the Boss makes. If organizers want to learn that information, they should contact their committee. When the organizers inoculate the people they're trying to organize, then the Boss move is half as effective at its goals of eroding support or damaging relationships.

In each subsequent Campaign Stage, the Boss or Decision Maker will gain a supplemental bundle of Cash or Public Capital that represents the income made from the workers' labor or alliances in the community. Each kind of employer will have a differing amount of income based on the industry and the flow of liquid assets to which the Boss has access.

Each Campaign Stage will also detail how much Cash or Public Capital the Boss gets to resupply with and the ways in which it can be used.

Campaign Playbook: While the overall structure of Campaign Stages can be adopted to many different industries, it may not prepare organizers for the variety of campaigns they could encounter. Other organizers and other union locals are welcome to use their existing training materials to create their own campaign playbooks. If you've picked up this game on a lark to see what union organizing is like, you can find more complete campaign books at PracticalFox.com

Ask Questions

Ask the organizer to your left, right, and across from you questions from the list below, or be inspired to use other questions based on the answers you get. These questions should begin an interview about the goals, origin, and destination of the organizer you are playing. The GM should pay close attention to the answers and prepare to plug these juicy details back into the narrative. A compelling story is one that aims at the organizers while they are trying to aid the workers.

Concerning Class War
- What role do you feel best suited for and why?
- How did you get into organizing?
- What was your first exposure to injustice?
- What has capital taken away from you? What has it given you?
- How did your worst boss treat you?

Concerning Sentiment
- Who on the team evokes the strongest emotion from you? Why?
- When we get a ride from you, what will shock us in your car?
- Who do you call each night after debrief?
- How does your family feel about your work?
- What would you do if you were not organizing?

Concerning Politics
- What does organizing mean to you personally?
- What is the most aggressive action you've ever been a part of? Who organized it?

- Who is your organizing role model?
- Where are you on the political spectrum?

Concerning Connections
- Who do you see regularly that works in the internal department of the local? Where and why?
- Who do you see in the political department of the local? How do you feel about them?
- Who do you know in a community organization that regularly attends actions? How did that relationship start?
- Who do you interact with most often that fills the office assistant role at the union? What favor do you own them?

SHARE
Share your organizer with the group. Introduce them by name. Tell your friends what they look like and their place in the local. What are their aspirations?

UNION ORGANIZATION
Much like other social organizations (clubs, churches, fraternal organizations, nonprofits, etc.) each union local has its own quirks and character. Most locals have a structure for members to direct their business. A union local's constitution will determine its officers and

authority figures. Don't get into these weeds. If you make the organization broadly determined, you'll have enough detail to run the game. If you're using this for training, you already know the structure of your local.

Each local could have:

- Elected President
- Elected Executive Director
- Elected Board of Directors
- Internal Department (business agents, reps or some other term)
- External Department (may be part of internal organizer's work)
- Political Department
- Communications Department
- Facilities Department

.

CPSIA information can be obtained
at www.ICGtesting.com
Printed in the USA
FFHW011759100319
50944648-56375FF